MW01232332

# Dark Psychology Secrets &

# Manipulation Techniques

The ultimate Blueprint to Master Mental Manipulation,

Mind Control, Human Psychology and Behavior,

Persuasion, and Emotional Intelligence to Get What you

Want from Anybody Part-1

# Tony Mathews

## Table of Contents

By reading this document, the reader agrees that under no circumstances is the author responsible for any losses, direct or indirect, which are incurred as a result of the use of information contained within this document, including, but not limited to, — errors, omissions, or inaccuracies.

# *Chapter #1*

# *The Concept of Dark*

# *Psychology*

## Introduction:

Psychology is the examination of how individuals think, feel and react to different conditions subject to the excited, physical and mental parts that accept a vocation in choosing a person's lead. Dark Psychology covers those components and segments that are normally difficult to look at with others, ungainly to surrender that we need assistance with regulating (from time to time expertly or therapeutically) and even deny exist since they are unreasonably malicious or frightening to perceive. The going with segments will discuss focuses related to Dark Psychology and affecting people, for instance, The claim to fame of impact and the different sorts of techniques that consolidates like Stealthy Impact and Dark Impact procedures The wide extent of mental techniques that are granulating ceaselessly on the planet consistently and how to spot them.

Capable tips and misdirects related to the perception and acing of Dark Psychology from authorities around the world relatable occurrences of intellectually manipulative and amazing techniques in veritable conditions the best strategy to recognize heartless direct and straightforward the dividers and shroud people opening up behind when they light have you anytime expected to acknowledge how people get others to hold tight their every word and follow every one of their propositions? Have you contemplated how factions that have all the earmarks of being so perilous and undermining when being seen from the outside make sense of how to draw in people to make their feelings and their isolated system more grounded? The usage of mental techniques, for instance, impact, control, and instilling is just a little bit of how these sorts of predators and Expert Controllers manage others and use them to propel their own destinations and lifestyle improvement.

## What is Dark Psychology:

Understanding why individuals are how we are having been a subject of enthusiastic, philosophical, social and mental investigation in some structure since people became mindful through development. Our capacity to fathom, to envision and to change the manner in which ourselves as well as other people see the world through slight adjustments in intuition or seeing are only a portion of the stunning gifts that the human cerebrum is prepared to do. With all the great parts of life that are supported by and the entirety of the creations created from the human psyche, numerous individuals waver to consider the shadowy side of human idea, feeling, and conduct and how it comes from the wondrous mental organ that keeps the remainder of the body running as it should.

In spite of the individuals who would prefer not consider the darker side of humankind, there are those in the realm of psychology that have committed their lives to:
Distinguishing qualities and enthusiastic characteristics Checking and considering singular practices Understanding perspectives and meanings of the world foreseeing hazardous or unsafe practices people might have the capacity to do to

themselves or others utilizing the data assembled over many years of study to all the more likely comprehend dark character types and make profiles dependent on past practices trying to show signs of improvement generally comprehension of the criminal psyche. Probably the most notable and regarded utilizes for psychology in human culture include:

Building better groups in work, sports, examine groups or whatever other control where individuals need to depend on one another so as to accomplish an objective building more grounded associations with loved one's gratitude to a more prominent comprehension of passionate reactions improved conciliatory relations between nations through upgraded correspondence and exchange aptitudes expanding profitability in workplaces or other expert settings Psychological well-being understanding and improvement.

# Treatment of enthusiastic and mental conditions:

Dark Psychology as there are territories to concentrate inside the subject. Utilize it or shield yourself from it when you think about the kind of individuals, conditions, circumstances, articulations, and activities to look out for. We'll be beginning our excursion through the darker side of the human brain by investigating the idea of Dark Psychology, its history and the various components that make it one of the most entrancing themes identified with the mind and how it takes a shot at the most basic and private levels.

The subject of psychology is one that catches the consideration of millions around the globe and has gotten significant in issues of both wellbeing and equity. Sadly, psychology additionally has an adverse cloud around it that causes individuals to delay before confiding in their own mental wellbeing and worries to the aptitude of others. Much of the time, this dithering originates from absence of commonality or comprehension with what psychology is and in what manner can be utilized every day to improve individuals' day by day lives. The investigation of psychology has had a huge effect on human mindfulness and comprehension of feelings, yet the subject in general reaches far more noteworthy and has a lot more prominent effect on our day by day lives than many give it acknowledgment for.

Psychology is characterized as the investigation of the science behind the musings, feelings and activities that administer every human dependent on their very own history or tendency toward scholarly or created practices. At the end of the day, individuals who study psychology are driven by interest and mission for information concerning why individuals are how we are. Dark Psychology brings that review into the shrouded pieces of the human brain, the territories that individuals attempt to disregard, to cover or to cover (on the off chance that they are even mindful of them). Others utilize their nature with dark mental techniques so as to impact the considerations of others, oversee others or control individuals into doing what they're told, now and then while never speculating their contemplations or activities weren't their own. Probably the most ordinarily read about and talked about sub-areas of Dark Psychology include:

## Cyberstalking and other virtual ruthless conduct:

This classification likewise incorporates characters as mellow as web trolls via web-based networking media locales to the most serious like virtual personality criminals political psychology falls into the domain of Dark Psychology, contingent upon who the subject of study is social psychology majors invest a considerable measure of energy contemplating the characteristics of Dark Psychology and how they can impact the conduct of various kinds of individuals there are various Dark Psychology techniques at use and by and by with those utilization the craft of self-advancement to improve their professions. The individuals who have made enduring signs of media outlets and the individuals who rule numerous imaginative professions have expressed gratitude toward mental strategies of influence and perusing individuals for encouraging their accomplishment in their picked fields.

Every individual's involvement in Dark Psychology in their own life all relies upon a person's character and on the off chance that they're simply the sort to attempt to shield from being the casualties of dark mental techniques or on the off chance that they're the sort to utilize them on others as a method for propelling their own position, profiting by a specific circumstance or purposely causing hurt.

## Dark Psychology History and impacts on Modern World:

In the event that Dark Psychology is such a subject of intrigue, for what reason is it despite everything considered such another and scarcely settled part of the mental world? While psychology in general is as yet a fresher idea where the historical backdrop of medication is concerned, Dark Psychology as a field of study is one of the most current advancements inside psychology since its acknowledgment into standard society as a genuine subject.

Dark Psychology positively shaped the field in the mid-2000s when clinicians everywhere throughout the world got decided and headed to all the more likely comprehend cybercriminals started assembling information that had been gathered on criminal psychology and profiling individuals so as to help get them or foresee their next assaults before they at any point got an opportunity to set them off. Examination into the individual characteristics related with Dark Psychology (otherwise called the qualities of perniciousness) has continued for a considerable length of time, prompting the absolute most noteworthy improvements foul play and criminal law over the globe, for example, Criminal profiling and insightful parts of administration devoted to its examination and upgrade at levels of government from district level cops to global analytical units' New laws set up shielding individuals from the most malevolent among us that might not have had the option to be managed by law previously expanding discipline sentences for the most pernicious or getting them clinical and mental treatment for their conditions that were not perceived by clinical or lawful circles in the years prior to a specific occasion today, Dark Psychology is of most popular as being specifically noteworthy to those contemplating the brains, musings, and activities of crooks that work inside the virtual domain for commonsense use and worldwide advantage. There have been incalculable utilizations made for it in the amusement business that keeps on being investigated remembering high caliber and useful shows for genuine violations cases to anecdotal crooks and wrongdoing solvers with profundity and acculturating characteristics that have grabbed the eye of individuals in all money, expert, social and class levels far and wide. More than everything else, Dark Psychology and its developing fame have constrained even those in the most forswearing about the darker side of human instinct to stand up and pay heed, tolerating that there is the chance of darker

attributes making themselves known in even the most joyful and idealistic of individuals. Every individual is made of up both constructive and pessimistic attributes, qualities and practices that are propelled or planned by the occasions we endure and the individuals we encircle ourselves with. It's superbly normal for every individual to have inquiries concerning their temperament, their considerations, their feelings and activities that can be replied by the examination and studies being done in the region of Dark Psychology.

## Effects of Dark Psychology on Human Beings:

There are nine-character characteristics that therapists most generally relate to the individuals who do well with Dark Psychology for individual use or as a subject of study all through their own and private lives. At times known as the

Attributes of Malignance, these character markers make up the establishments of darker characters and understanding them can help with distinguishing their utilization around you, deliberate or obscure.

Having only one of the characteristics recognizable isn't sufficient for somebody to decidedly be marked a dark character. On the off chance that they just fall into one classification of markers, at that point it could simply be an opportunity advancement from some energetic injury or troublesome situation they endure that ended up having a significant impact on the formation of that person's character. In cases like these where the quality is destructive to the individual or to other people, or where the individual can't acknowledge this piece of themselves and it prompts other mental troubles, the individual should look for the assistance of an analyst or other mental human services proficient to recognize their interests and make sense of together how best to treat them pushing ahead.

Here is a more intensive glance at those qualities showed by and recognized in individuals with darker characters who are driven by their own Dark Psychology.

1.    **Narcissism:** Narcissists are person's whose activities, contemplations and concerns rotate around their own prosperity and progression before others, now and again to the detriment of others. This character attribute is roused by the Greek fantasy of Narcissus, a man who squandered his life in affection with his own appearance. Narcissists tend to not function admirably in gatherings and can be handily irritated on the off chance that others attempt to regulate them.

2.    **Overly Delicate Inner selves:** Likewise, usually alluded to as Egomaniacs, individuals with excessively touchy personalities can appear to be like Narcissists on paper, however there is a key distinction between the two. Like Narcissists, individuals with excessively touchy personalities are generally centered around their own progression and improvement throughout everyday life, except not at all like Narcissists who have a normally high assessment of themselves, Egomaniacs and other people who show this trademark decide their self-commendable dependent on what others consider them. At the point when others praise them, their self-esteem increments and they can work without drawing in an excessive amount of consideration in their environment, regardless of whether that is busy working or at

home. It's when Narcissists and those with excessively touchy inner selves get denounced or censured that their darker nature turns out and it can show is various ways, as dormancy or hostile to social practices.

3.    **Inflated Personal responsibility**: Individuals with swelled personal circumstances are additionally centered around their own advancement and prosperity, to the point of strolling over or forsaking others. This trademark is frequently joined forces with eminent individual desire and drive that makes them stand apart among their companions. Lamentably, similar to Narcissists and individuals with excessively delicate self-images, they don't do well in group or gathering situations yet will in general exceed expectations in positions of authority and overseeing others as long as they have somebody to reply to that has an increasingly nonpartisan or adjusted character and standard of conduct.

4.    **Personal Qualification:** Individuals who are for the most part and by and by entitled accept that they are owed things right now. While the points of interest fluctuate from individual to singular, individuals who are entitled feel that they merit what they see others have. It could be shallow like belongings or the measure of cash someone else makes. It

could be more profound like inclination that they merit love and regard without winning it or quest for it as a great many people do. Their darker natures turn out when they believe they have been denied something that as they would like to think they're qualified for.

Privilege that is utilized in inquiring about the attribute is that of ruined youngsters. Qualification is a scholarly characteristic that numerous individuals develop out of in their high school years astonishingly into adulthood, yet it very well may be energized or incited by components, for example, monetary standing, social class and individual achievement (or disappointment, contingent upon the individual conditions).

5.    **Manipulative Inclinations:** Individuals who harp on the dark side of psychology are known for having an ability for control. This might be as mellow as utilizing a present for control to ensure they have the best deals numbers every week to the individuals who utilize their aptitudes for political progression and wind up driving others through idea control and different perilous techniques.

Frequently called the Ambitious characteristic, the individuals who show capability for mental control of others for their own benefit are named after the political scholar Niccolò Machiavelli. Machiavelli's political convictions were based around the possibility that the methods used to accomplish a specific objective are constantly worth the methods (regularly paying little mind to the expense or harm done, as long as it doesn't adversely influence the person being referred to).

6. **Moral Withdrawal:** This is the expression normally used to depict the individuals who have a perspective on world and how it is administered and truly accepts that the standards set up don't concern them. Individuals who have this character attribute are known for intuition they are over the principles and are thusly ready to talk or take activities that others would think about dishonest or wrong without feeling any sort of good obligation, blame or disgrace afterward.

7. **Psychopathy and Psychopathic Propensities:** Somebody who is has been a marked a maniac has been recognized by proficient therapists or character specialists as having a character issue called

psychopathy, in which an individual is inadequate in sympathy or regret for anybody or anything. "Psychopath" has entered the normal tongue as a notable engaging word for sequential executioners and different crooks that fall into that character type. They've been put on the map in TV arrangement and blood and gore films; however, this is one of the more misconstrued attributes that is as yet being characterized and concentrated as increasingly more is found about the psychopathic brain.

8. **Sadism and Vicious Practices:** A twisted person is somebody who has been recognized as demonstrating cruel examples of conduct or show as a component of their shaped character a propensity for making torment or embarrassment others (and picking up delight from these activities) as a method for affirming their capacity and authority over others. The mischief doesn't generally need to be physical or mental. This character attribute is regularly associated with sexual control just as passionate and mental force declaration.

9. **Spitefulness and Pernicious Inclinations:** Vindictiveness is the knowing and ability to cause hurt or do abhorrence and disdain is the readiness to make this move or

this mischief regardless of whether it implies hurting themselves all the while (genuinely, sincerely or mentally).

# *Chapter #2*

# *Who Uses Dark Psychology to Influence People?*

## Identify Predator Before Becoming Victim:

At the point when individuals hear "predator", numerous naturally consider jaguars stalking littler creatures through the trees or picture lines of extremely sharp teeth from a meat -eating dinosaur painting from their youth exhibition hall trip recollections. While the facts demonstrate that the term is normally saved for creatures that are known for chasing, the real meaning of a predator covers more than creature intuition. Predators are characterized as creatures that normally go after or abuse others for their own advantage. On account of creatures, this is essentially the meaning of the Hover of Life or the normal request of things. It is justifiable that so as to endure, a few species feed on different species. This idea possibly becomes disrupting when endurance is removed from the condition, and the creature being referred to (on account of Dark Psychology and its investigations, a person) is going after and misusing others for its delight or out of greedy.

A recognizable range of abilities for the craft of misdirection is a typical quality among predators, the subtleties of which we will cover all the more completely all through this section. Of all the character types recognized in the exploration of Dark Psychology, the predator is one of the most regularly found and the most hazardous whenever left unmonitored. Find a good pace savage sort, a portion of their best deceives for everyday use and how to shield yourself from them when they cajole their way into environment (or even into your trust).

## Spot Human Predators:

Human Predators are individuals who have no issue (ethically, genuinely or mentally) with making life hard for other people, particularly when the aftereffects of the activity make life simpler for themselves simultaneously. Only one out of every odd predator has a similar thought process, drive, objective or strategy so it is imperative to know how a portion of the more predominant sorts of Human Predators and instructions to distinguish them with the goal that you are prepared regardless of when or where you experience these individuals.

**Social Predator:** A Social Predator is somebody who is driven by a craving to defeat each impediment and sees everything from an inviting round of catch to an organization game as a basic serious obstacle for them to win. Their need to succeed at everything makes mingling hard for them and their swelled inner selves are effectively wounded, especially whenever addressed before their companions or individuals they see as substandard. One of the most habitually displayed character characteristics of Social Predators is their base want to succeed at everything. This could be in genuine issues, for example, setting up strength in a room loaded with associates or it could be in basic discussions, for example, casual discussion in a lift. They are keen on their own headway in both individual and expert issues and consider them to be to their objectives as being accomplished by improving their social standing or making significant associations that could be depended upon in the midst of battle. The vast majority meet Social Predators in the work environment, turning into the casualty of their verbal and mental maltreatment at the workplace. While their assurance and eye for subtleties make individuals, who group as Social Predators possibly proficient and beneficial representatives, they don't cooperate with other people, making group activities or occasions inconceivability's without impressive exchange or on the other hand conduct observing from somebody they recognize as prevalent. While it is less normal, Social Predators can show savage disposition changes and truly damaging conduct in their own, private and sentimental experiences.

**Sexual Stalker:** A Sexual Stalker is somebody who deals with someone else or their contemplations and activities through sexual triumph, frequently by truly, intellectually or mentally malignant methods. The expression "Sexual Stalker" is regularly connected with grown-ups who target kids, win their trust and afterward go after their youthfulness and absence of common experience to exploit them for individual addition or fulfillment. Predators get their name from their bestial or basic behaviorisms and methods for survey their kindred people. One recognizable trademark that is related with predators is the means by which they pick their prey or chasing grounds. Social Predators for instance can utilize their deliberately created social aptitudes to work their techniques in practically any settings. Sexual Stalkers then again are better ready to place their specializations enthusiastically in recognizable and controlled settings, focusing on a particular sort of individual or chain of occasions.

The term initially came to use in the standard culture in the mid-1980s and is normally put something aside for the individuals who not exclusively are known to chase like predators through sexual implies however have likewise been recorded as submitting an explicitly fierce act before. Virtual, Digital or Online Predator: This classification of predators alludes to those individuals who exploit others for their own benefit using innovation and mechanical progressions like internet-based life, online visit gatherings, dating applications, network board locales, and an apparently interminable rundown of virtual tricks. Data fraud is one of the most usually talked about virtual violations submitted by

Digital Predators. The way toward demonstrating it very well may be exhausting and it can take a long time to recuperate from monetarily and where credit is concerned.

This is one of the ruthless social sorts that those captivated in examining Dark Psychology pick a subject of research or point by point intrigue. Digital Predators are a developing worry as increasingly more of our everyday lives become advanced or virtual from getting paid to set aside cash for retirement, discussing safely with loved ones to sharing fragile data in basic circumstances unafraid of it being taken, caught or duplicated. Because of the way that all correspondence with Digital Predators is done basically, it tends to be about difficult to find these hoodlums and hazardous people or gatherings that utilization the web as a boundless chasing ground. A considerable lot of the new headways in cybersecurity intended to ensure the powerless or new to virtual communications can likewise be utilized to shield and secure the individuals who are utilizing the virtual world for detestable methods.

**Passionate Predator:** This kind of predator is frequently generalized with the likes of general predators who are as yet being prepared for an increasingly explicit classification. They are characterized as individuals who feel positive and pleasured by making hurt others. What explicitly isolates Enthusiastic Predators from a general order of those with ruthless conduct is that their normal chasing ground includes exploited people that are focused for their sentimental relationship potential. Enthusiastic Predators construct sentimental connections not out of a craving for friendship yet so as to profit here and there whether it is from centered passionate and mental mischief after some time as the relationship develops or the advantage could likewise be money related, with the predator shaping a relationship so as to separate from their mate later for financial increase. There is an assortment of other savage names that individuals can be given, contingent upon their practices and their definitive rationale in the techniques they flawless through training or the individuals they focus in their supported chasing grounds. The most ideal approach to secure yourself and your loved ones from predators isn't to retain all the various sorts, but instead to comprehend the general markers that can be utilized to recognize somebody flaunting ruthless considerations and activities. It's generally said that information is power, or at the end of the day, the more an individual knows, the more effective and profitable they will be all through their undertakings or in arriving at their own and expert objectives. The equivalent is valid for those intrigued by Dark Psychology, its influence the human brain and especially how to recognize predators in their environment or individual life.

## What is a Human Predator?

As legitimate and mindful individuals, the vast majority comprehend and can see the distinction in that taking prey for endurance is the method for the world, yet that exploiting progressively helpless individuals or animals when life isn't on the line isn't right. Predators (paying little mind to what sub-area of arrangement they fall into) can't make this qualification and are not worried by the way that they don't understand this as the normal individual does. A Human Predator is somebody who utilizes their comprehension of human wants, thought control, and the general mental condition of each individual they meet to consistently realize how to control and exploit them when the opportunity arrives. Human Predators don't make associations with others except if there is some approach to profit by that relationship, either by accomplishing a specific objective or by securing something they need or need. There is a scope of various kinds of Human Predators that have been recognized, however there are innumerable investigations being performed far and wide that are attempting to limit the meanings of predator bunches so as to increase a superior comprehension of how to treat or handle them if treatment isn't a choice. Specialists additionally study human instinct and new discoveries that are printed each looking for recognizing and characterizing other potential ruthless characters, activities or practices that could be utilized to forestall or catch predators before they can make irreversible mischief themselves as well as other people.

There are a perpetual number of conditions that can cause a passionate response in people. Utilizing long periods of study in psychology and the more explicit fields, for example, Dark Psychology, specialists have devoted their lives and professions to responding to the subject of whether it is conceivable to foresee how individuals will respond. The accompanying outline shows a rundown of basic human practices on the left and the most usually announced responses in regions of both live testing and boundless emotional well-being studies.

## Art of Deception:

When they have selected their injured individual, the following stage for them is to procure the unfortunate casualty's trust and afterward use strategies for misdirection so as to oversee them to accomplish their objective. Characterized, misdirection is the demonstration of misleading somebody or causing them to accept or even help an announcement or other data that isn't valid. At the point when it goes from being a straightforward activity to being named craftsmanship, somebody has drilled and built up their misleading aptitudes to a point that their demonstration is consistent, watertight, and viable for accomplishing the objectives they planned them for. Regular instances of double -dealing individuals may run into in their everyday lives include:

Kids are acceptable at gentle double dealing, especially when they believe they are in a tough situation or realize they have accomplished something incorrectly. One of the most utilized beguiling techniques utilized by youngsters is the "vexed stomach" or "excruciating gut". By pretending a sickness that is terrible enough to keep them from doing or discussing whatever they are attempting to maintain a strategic distance from, they discover that as long as they don't need to guarantee anything awful enough that it would require a specialist, they can utilize this as a powerful methods for trickery for an assortment of conditions (accepting they don't get captured).

The morals of clinical investigations and the utilization of fake treatments has been raised doubt about on whether it is correct, compelling for getting solid outcomes, or a technique for explore that ought to be considered due to the beguiling nature and potential impact on the outcomes. A fake treatment is a sugar-based pill that is marked as another sort of real medication that is being tried and given to half of the guineas pigs at a similar recurrence of the cured half to perceive how the concoction make-up of the genuine medication influences the human structure contrasted with the impacts felt by those taking the fake treatment.

The "Harmless embellishment" is another regular misleading method that individuals use for an assortment of reasons. An innocent embellishment an explanation that is false or misleading yet said so as to forestall the destructive enthusiastic or mental impacts that reality would have on a person. Instances of this incorporate telling a colleague that you like the new outfit they're wearing as a method for boosting their certainty despite the fact that it may not be a style you appreciate or telling a customer that the absurd measure of detail work they had you do to bring a deal to a close was no issue despite the fact that you needed to place in three hours of additional time. Predators of any sort are risky as their primary objective in life is to make hurt others for their own vanity, rise or improvement. For the individuals who see these practices or character-characterizing qualities in their companions, friends and family or the individuals they work with, the best way to guarantee you are protected from the grip of a predator and shield from turning into an injured individual is to expel them or yourself from any closeness or commonality with them. It tends to be surprisingly troublesome, contingent upon close you are to the individual or how constrained you are in moves you can make to control the circumstance, however it is well justified, despite all the trouble, at last, to ensure the conservation of your own psychology, mental and enthusiastic status all through the entirety of life's good and bad times.

# *Chapter #3*

# *Ways to spot Deception*

**Quiet and Mindful:** This is a typical nature of predators and the people who use Dark Psychology techniques in order to encourage their own or master standing. The central clarification behind this is in order to find deficiencies and vulnerabilities in people, errands or conditions, you should have a solid understanding of what\'s going on around you. The more information an individual can amass about their condition or the people that they are locked in with, the more they have to use to further their potential benefit whenever the open door shows up. People who use intimidation as a strategy for getting money or run cons are known for being worthy crowd individuals and mindful watchers by the people who knew them already or during their criminal exhibitions. These sorts of people are normally portrayed as being mavericks due to their spared nature, anyway fit even more eagerly away from any limiting impact Character characterization as they can move energetically among pulled back and cordial depending upon what their present needs are.

**The Risk Is in The Nuances:** Predators that deal in cons or social stunts, for instance, theft from concentrated events rely upon dubiousness and lies in order to go without getting caught or hindered in their plans. Studies done on an overall scale and over a variety mature enough get-togethers show that one social inclination for people that have honed their aptitudes in trickiness is that when they have to lie in order to achieve their targets, they put in as barely any nuances as could be normal the situation being what it is. For example, they may tell someone that they can\'t get together with them later in light of the fact that they\'re going out, yet they will disregard nuances like what time they will be out or where unequivocally they will be going. The clarification behind this is because nuances can be checked and they can be tested.

**Keep It Essential and Direct:** The best admonishment most masters offer to those wanting to develop their powers of confusion isn't to anxiously or straightforwardly give information or bits of knowledge concerning anything you\'re doing. Perhaps instruct people with respect to what\'s going on when they ask and cause a point to simply answer what they to ask. Keep it questionable and keep it clear. Logically erratic stories are progressively difficult to review and far more straightforward to get caught in if they are false.

**Excess and Buying Time:** It may make someone sound like a parrot in case they are being met or questioned, anyway one social affinity that the people who practice Dark

# Dark Psychology Secrets & Manipulation Techniques

Psychology either stop by ordinarily or learn as an instilled intuition is the show of repeating tends to they are asked before taking note of them or reiterating huge bits of information (normally in their own words) to ensure there is no misguided judgment and moreover to guarantee that they simply respond to accurately what has been asked of them. Thusly they can avoid coincidentally letting any extra or possible accursing information slip.

Emphasis is another lead inclination shared by the people who moreover show characteristics of psychopathy and still making social capacities. Exactly when used by these sorts of characters, excess can moreover be named mimicry. In repeating the tone and the particular wording of the people who address them first, they can practice their own tone and wording as they develop an individual style and vitality that will end up being an essential factor in their undeniably complex Dark Psychology techniques and plans. Not only are they expanding commonsense association right now, yet they can in like manner be sure that the style they're making is normal stood out from other human lead and social qualities.

**Physical Ticks and Giveaways:** When asked their contemplations on an energetic topic or got some data about something individual and sensitive, precarious people will as a rule inhale simple in light of negligent physical ticks that can be used as giveaways for those looking for deceiving attributes. Presumably the most noted deceiving ticks include:

Playing with their hair either by turning it in their fingers or running their hands through it to brush it away from their face (whether or not there is nothing there) extended heartbeat and heavier breathing are in like manner fundamental signs of craftiness tinkering with gets or pulling at their articles of clothing when thinking or listening carefully to what is being discussed anyway don\'t want to take a gander at the people around them the individual improvements or inclinations that people show will move from individual to individual the best approach to acing the claim to fame of recognizing misdirecting is practicing you're watching and blending capacities Arranged to get acquainted with Dark Psychology and the different sorts of techniques people use while practicing or considering this psychological field? Keep examining to learn not exactly what kind of grouping there is of systems and exercises to be developed, yet moreover how to recognize these techniques when they are used on you and how to shield yourself from transforming into a setback of savage direct.

# *Chapter #4*

# *The Dark Psychology of*

# *Persuasion*

As a typical correspondence expertise, there is nothing essentially amiss with the specialty of influence. All things considered, that is the means by which we persuade individuals to help our causes or to join our side of a contention. Salespeople in each industry use influence strategies to advance their items over their rivals and lawmakers use them to carry voters to their side before a political race. Needing others to be our ally is a characteristic human feeling identified with our base requirement for socialization with others, having individuals around us that we currently have our backs and being loved by the individuals who may have bounced to negative ends dependent on appearance or the surprising occasions of a circumstance that may have given them a errible initial introduction. Notwithstanding, when utilized for loathsome or vindictive purposes, influence goes in a new direction and turns into a hazardous apparatus for compulsion and taking bit of leeway of others. This is the place even a fundamental comprehension of Dark and Undercover Influence strategies can prove to be useful for the individuals who have battled with succumbing to great influence procedures before. Right now, investigate influence as a mental strategy for control and in general with the goal that peruses have a superior handle of influence from the definition and idea to recognizable proof and assurance.

## What is Persuasion?

Influence is characterized as the deliberate procedure of impacting others by giving data, shaping a battle or visual energizer that intended to adjust their musings and sentiments, or through inconspicuous compulsion. Now and again, the pressure is subliminal and truly it must be with the end goal for influence to be completely compelling. Individuals can attempt to convince others that they are morally justified or that they realize the most ideal approach to achieve an undertaking, however simply telling others (even bolstered by realities, experience, and information) can prompt contentions and hatred. The way to influence is having the option to get somebody to convince themselves utilizing the contentions, data or pictures they've been given by the individual attempting to do the convincing.

Dark Influence is a mainstream point for individuals contemplating Dark Psychology just as a result of how predominant influence is in day by day worldwide correspondences. Dark Influence is likewise characterized as the demonstration of getting somebody to do, think, feel or think something through persuading them with data and contentions or by charming them to an idea or point through enthusiastic interests. The distinction between Dark Influence and influence by and large psychology is the thought process and drive behind the need to convince close by the general objective and expectation of the individual doing the convincing.

At the end of the day, individuals who practice general influence strategies might not have any sort of fundamental thought process in their crusades. This is regular in the publicizing business as individuals who are acceptable at influence are contracted to persuade individuals regarding something or to purchase something, yet never with any genuine expectation for additional control or control. The distinction can be hard to see, especially for the individuals who are themselves unpracticed with influence techniques or facing somebody who has aced (or verge on acing) the craft of influence. One stunt for the individuals who figure they might be affected by somebody rehearsing Dark Influence is to make a stride back and take a gander at the circumstance to check whether there is a potential greater picture impacting everything. General mental influence typically just has one objective: prevail upon somebody so they purchase your item, take up a reason or join your side in a contention. Dark

Influence will consistently make plans and techniques a stride further.

The individuals who rehearse and depend on Dark Influence strategies and techniques never simply need somebody to alter their perspectives and leave it at that. There is constantly a further drive or expectation behind their influence strategies. This can be anything from guaranteeing their help when others attempt to go up against them or so as to get them to make a move that they themselves need to maintain a strategic distance from in light of the fact that it is risky or shameless and could hurt their own notoriety. The rudiments are that, as with most territories of Dark Psychology, individuals who practice Dark Influence consider other to be as instruments or as a necessary chore so as to better their lives or their standing.

## Dark Persuasion Versus Covert Persuasion?

"Covert" has a method for making individuals immediately suspicious and reluctant to part in circumstances or strategies. Others naturally consider super government agents like James Bond and the undercover activities such characters are renowned for. The meaning of clandestine is an idea, method or activity that is performed with no immediate affirmation or with any observer or real sight.

Clandestine Influence has no good or moral issues or thought processes, likewise with Dark Influence, yet rather covers those techniques for general influence that focus on their crowd's capacity to convince them over to their side without them consistently realizing they had been the objective of a fruitful influence battle and made up their own personalities. While individuals who practice Dark Influence can utilize techniques distinguished and remembered for the specialty of Clandestine Influence, the secret strategies all alone are not viewed as dark or exploitative. Recognizing the distinction between the two comes down to having the option to decide thought process and purpose behind the influence techniques. Ask yourself these inquiries when you believe you're being convinced or when you feel constrained to alter your perspective (and are not exactly sure why):

Is it perilous or conceivably unsafe in any capacity? Who profits by this? Is there any individual explicitly or might it be able to conceivably profit a bigger gathering of individuals? Do I believe this individual and how they are addressing me or introducing their contention? Have they said anything excruciating or annoying? Have they done or said whatever focused your confidence or assessment of yourself? Do I have the data I have to settle on an educated choice? What other data would it be a good idea for me to search for before making any sort of move right now?

Basic Circumstances for Conceivably Dark Enticing Conduct to Flourish One technique for influence (Dark, Secretive or something else) is the understanding strategy. This method sits at the very center of mental influence considers and is a decent beginning activity for those new to the specialty of influence to make a propensity for. Essentially, when the objective has been recognized, the objective has been resolved and an arrangement has been authorized, the following strategy for somebody attempting to convince others is to concur with each word that leaves their mouths. Regardless of whether it is irrational to getting them on your side, concurring with individuals manufactures trust (a basic component of fruitful influence). The most significant guideline for the individuals who need to begin rehearsing this technique is that the objective is in every case right. In any event, when you realize they are incorrect, they are correct. It can sound confounding, yet essentially what this implies when you are attempting to convince somebody of something and they can't help contradicting you or state something erroneous, rather than going up against them or getting down on them about it and mentioning to them what is right or what you need them to accept, you figure out how to modify their perspective first by concurring with them and afterward utilizing other inconspicuous influence techniques to get them to change their perspective. The individual contradicting the persuader or saying something that is conflicting to a definitive objective of the influence plan is a reasonable sign that the influence strategies utilized so far have not been fruitful and the arrangement may require adjusting. This is the place having a psychological tool kit loaded up with influence strategies is acceptable (even critical) for the individuals who use it or need to begin rehearsing it in their own lives.

Mechanical advancements are specifically compelling to the individuals who practice enticing conduct. The fundamental explanations behind this are innovation (purchased for individual or expert use) is around us consistently. From PDAs in everybody's pockets or sacks to TVs on the dividers in basically every café, sitting tight for a territory or other space where individuals assemble to take a break together or all alone. This is additionally one reason that the promoting business is such a mainstream goal for the individuals who realize they have an ability for influence. With regards to sharing recordings, pictures or news cuts, nothing ventures quicker than an interesting advertisement or superstar support shared via web-based networking media or sent as a private message for individuals to impart to loved ones. Innovation has opened the world for the influential (and predators of various sorts) and made it simpler for them to grow their intended interest groups and general chasing grounds. The uplifting news for potential unfortunate casualties is that a bigger assortment of individuals to go after methods an increasingly differing and repudiating assortment of individuals they have to prevail upon. This implies convincing individuals have new difficulties, not in really contacting individuals as that has gotten perhaps the most straightforward piece of any Dark Mental control technique on account of steady web access and portable innovation, yet in reality prevailing upon individuals as one crusade or contention may not associate with some the manner in which it does with others.

## Popular Persuasion Techniques:

One of the most widely recognized Secretive Influence strategies at use in both individual and expert circles is comprehension of the "10,000-foot view". Regardless of what the circumstance, the points of interest, or the ultimate objective, seeing how the objective recalls their past encounters as well as imagines their future. This strategy is especially viable for the individuals who have an objective that is on the negative side of their contention and should be convinced to the positive side to either pick up help or close a deal. Individuals are bound to be available to influence and tolerating other data or activities as gainful in the event that they feel the individual they're conversing with gets them and considers them to be an individual (instead of an objective). Social aptitudes, relational abilities, sympathy and the capacity to interpret words and activities as a person's passionate reactions are on the whole other fundamental human association capacities that are a great idea to have involvement in when attempting to convince somebody. Tune in to the individual's understanding and history with the subject you are attempting to convince them on identify locate some shared opinion so as to win their trust and make an individual association continuously ask them where they stand and for what good reason, they feel that route about your subject before attempting any influence techniques. This is a method for making a gauge or a beginning stage to improve building a compelling influence plan.

When their position has been built up, get some information about how they see the circumstance or contention wrapping up. This tells you which potential future they are imagining and how their optimal circumstance would end since you have a comprehension of their history and their vision of things to come (as it identifies with your theme), you can pick which further developed, secret or darker influence techniques can assist you with accomplishing your definitive objectives and resolve the circumstance with the future you have imagined or sought after the accompanying outline gives a visual presentation of how influence functions at its most basic level from the beginning stage (or probability of transformation) to the two primary ways an individual can choose to take starting there so as to alter somebody's perspective in their mind or until the other individual takes the activities that the persuader is seeking after. The best case of this tip in real life originates from the universe of rivalry and games. Most games are part into equal parts or have a various segment that groups or people need to perform effectively to be named the champ and beat out their rivals or contending groups. At the point when the main half or initial segment of a test turns out poorly, it doesn't really imply that the whole game is lost. It is anything but difficult to get disheartened when things are not going as arranged or somebody isn't proceeding as they trusted, especially on the off chance that they have been preparing for quite a while. This is whenever mentors have the chance to practice their influence capacities as a method for reigniting an energy or drive for the game in their disillusioned rivals before the remainder of the test or rivalry.

A typical contention for this is not performing admirably toward the start should just fill in as more motivation to help one's vitality and focus one's concentrated all the more seriously for the remainder of the test. A recharged drive and improved vitality levels (from loosening up sore muscles, rehydrating or expending some protein or other fuel) can have a significant effect in somebody's presentation and rely upon how a long ways behind the individual or group is, it very well may be the deciding variable for how to close the hole and afterward outperform their rivals so as to win the honor or game! On the off chance that there is more than one potential result for the individual being convinced, either by settling on a choice about a buy, someone else or a game-plan, and the two are similarly advantageous for themselves or for the persuader (contingent upon their thought processes and purpose) one system those with influence experience depend on is moving the objective's consideration between alternatives so they don't shape a passionate or mental association with one of them specifically. Regardless of whether there is no misfortune for the individual paying little mind to which choice they make, individuals will in general feel a feeling of misfortune and lament that can settle on them begin to scrutinize the choice they made and how they showed up at it. This is something that is useful for individuals turning out to be mindful and seeing that they have been the casualties of an influential arrangement or battle, yet not useful for those rehearsing and sharpening their influence techniques.

## Protect yourself from Dark Persuasion:

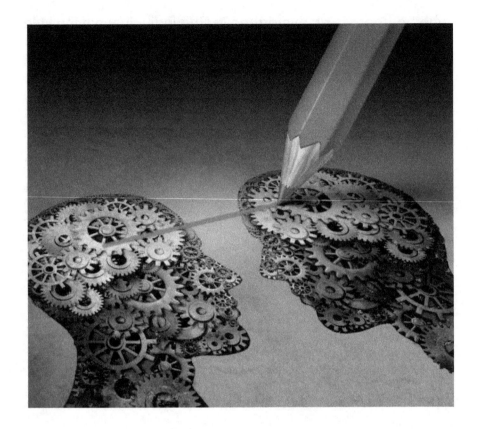

Sooner or later, everybody believes that they are insusceptible to influence, that they are either so acceptable at perusing individuals that they could never fall for a shallow pitch or that they are so sure in their musings, emotions, and convictions that they would never be influenced. In any case, in all actuality sooner or later in their lives, everybody gets convinced into altering their perspective on something whether it is by a companion who is attempting to persuade them to see a contention from their perspective (and does so effectively) or an influential promoting effort that prevails upon them from a brand they've been faithful to for quite a long time. They should be loved is something that most of humankind battles with sooner or later in their lives. We are especially inclined to changing our musings, convictions or practices in the midst of pressure or isolation, when we wind up in new environmental factors with new individuals (especially in the event that they are another sort of individual than we are familiar with managing and associating with all the time), and all through development from youth to the early long periods of adulthood. Numerous individuals recognize that they have done this sooner or later, generally in the center or secondary school when companion pressure shows signs of improvement of the vast majority. It is a lot simpler to perceive and lament sometime later that it is to recognize and modify your activities right now.

This is a characteristic human quality that individuals who use influence for darker purposes depend on, especially in the event that they are experiencing issues enchanting their way into an individual's trust and confidences. One of the primary drivers of the should be loved is low confidence or contrary closely-held conviction of oneself. This is a passionate shortcoming that makes every individual helpless against malevolent influence strategies yet can be taken into individual control and managed when an individual comprehends what it is about themselves or their lives that is causing such a low conclusion. The primary method to do this (and to abstain from turning into the casualty of an influence activity) is by rehearsing certainty building practices so as to fortify your faith in yourself and consistently have a psyche hungry for learning. This last part is significant as another reason for low self-esteem and defective independence is regularly because of an absence of data about a subject or an individual that we realize little to nothing about. All individuals structure suppositions dependent on what they see and hear regularly, and relying upon their Mental Character Type, they might be increasingly inclined to voicing their musings or feelings without knowing the full story. This not just offers individuals helpless against negative remarks from others and shame on the off chance that other people who have more information are fierce with them and they are not readied, yet it is likewise a factor that the individuals who realize how to utilize influence as a weapon or technique for control search for in the individuals they target.

Regardless of where you look, there is some type of influence being utilized and most of it is innocuous and can possibly be utilized to profit the entire of society whenever utilized with positive thought processes. With regards to influence, it is extremely just the hazardous factors and insights that you ought to be searching for, the pieces of influence that can be utilized as a method for control or achieving control over others. When you believe you're the casualty of noxious influence strategies and how to deal with them when they've been recognized. Is the individual or battle focusing on you to cause you to feel better than expected or exceptional in any capacity? This in itself may not be a marker of influential techniques, however it is one of the most well-known strategies put into impact. By causing somebody to feel exceptional, it helps their certainty and procures their trust, making them progressively open to powerful techniques. It is safe to say that they are offering conflicting expressions or continually stepping you back to the subject when you attempt to change the subject of discussion? This is an indication that somebody might be trying the positive understanding strategy so as to pick up trust and is unobtrusively attempting to keep you concentrated on their influence plan without really recognizing or conceding that they are attempting to control your musings and assessments.

Narrating is an incredible influence instrument for any individual who needs to make an enthusiastic association with their objective, particularly on the off chance that it is somebody they don't know by and by. There is nothing that joins individuals like a decent story and a decent story can be hard to see as an influence technique, particularly for the individuals who are simply mingling and don't think they are being impacted.

Most of information gathered, trust in your own capacities (regardless of whether it is for influence or for perceiving the truth about influence strategies) and level of influence aptitudes will accompany understanding and expanded mindfulness. There is no restriction of data and research on influence all in all psychology and Dark Psychology circles. Ideally, our guide has given you all that you have to begin with your own objectives for influence (paying little heed to what they might be), however never quit learning and consistently search out additional! Range of abilities and information on any theme or practice you check out for a mind-blowing duration.

# *Chapter #5*

# *Defining Dark Manipulation*

Ace Controllers, similar to the individuals who practice the craft of influence, have a wide range of levels, powers, thought processes and uses for their specific abilities that change from individual to individual. At the easiest level, controllers are individuals who can change their character, their friendliness, their suppositions or their perspective so as to make another person think some falsehood to the point of making a move or offering expressions that they could never manage without impact and not in any case addressing it.

Analysts everywhere throughout the world accept that every individual has three mental faces or sides to their character that characterize their distinction, decide their activities and structure the reason for every close to home association and connections began all through their lifetime:

The main face that individuals see when they see somebody is their open face, additionally in some cases called their open face. This character is the one they need individuals to see, the cover they are holing up behind to stay away from their own difficulties or shield themselves from enthusiastic mischief brought about by the dismissal or tormenting of others around them.

The subsequent face is the one that just those nearest to an individual find a good pace even find a good pace. This is simply the adaptation that is increasingly transparent gratitude to the security we search those we're generally OK with. Be that as it may, it is additionally part of a cover that individuals use so as to extend the character we need our nearest associations with grasp. Moving beyond this cover is the best way to manufacture dependable and unbreakable individual connections and this is the veil that is once in a while appeared by controllers, in any event, when they are not acting in a manipulative manner around the individuals they know and love.

The third (and generally sly) face is the one that nobody sees or ever finds a good pace, it's simply the face we don't appear out of dread or forswearing. This third face is the one that holds the outright certainties of our characters and when broke down (by and by or in mental treatment), can even give the responses to the individuals who are battling with finding what their identity is, a big motivator for they, what they accept and who they need to be. It is totally covered up by the mental covers produced for the other two appearances. It isn't until the last face has been recognized and comprehended by every individual that they can chip away at disposing of their surface mental covers on the initial two levels and permit themselves as well as other people to consider them to be they genuinely are.

With regards to this side of their individual characters, the individuals who are controllers or rehearsing their control aptitudes will need to get mindful of their thought processes, drives, and objectives associated with their actual being. The explanation behind this is simply the better understanding an individual has of themselves, the more mindful they are, the better manipulative veils they can make since they have a superior handle of their own temperament and can all the more likely spot (or even foresee) passionate reactions that could influence their movement or power over the circumstance they end up in. Having the option to utilize manipulative techniques for individual addition or having the option to recognize a controller so as to abstain from turning into an unfortunate casualty or potential objective beginnings with a total comprehension of control as an idea, as a training, as a character advancement device for developing characters and the various sorts control hypotheses and techniques grinding away in present day society.

Right now, will cover these themes alongside talking about other significant data identified with control, psychology and the darker side of human impact for individual use or individual insurance (contingent upon your expectation and thought processes).

## Manipulation in Psychology:

The meaning of control varies relying upon who is doing the characterizing. Frequently, it is characterized as the demonstration of getting somebody to do or say something through astute and handy impacting with respect to the controller. A few definitions even venture to show the absolute most observable characteristics and examples of mental control on that must be available in a person's conduct with their objectives or exploited people for them to merit the mark as a controller, for example, Undue constraining to the point of blame or uneasiness with respect to the person in question Mental, enthusiastic and mental mutilation to deal with contemplations and activities Conditional and individual abuse (or exploiting any shortcoming or opening they find in an individual or circumstance) Notwithstanding who you are conversing with and their own involvement in control and control procedures, most of individuals consequently associate the word with negative activities and now and then even pitiless techniques for impact that cause torment to other people and stunt them into doing things they could never do. Now and again, this perspective is exact and in considering the historical backdrop of control all through the human experience, anybody can perceive any reason why. Essentially it is a direct result of how dull and perilous manipulative individuals have demonstrated to be looking back when encounters are examined, and individuals are attempting to recapture control of their lives or mental and mental state.

All things considered, control (concerning human brain research) is a method for overseeing another person to accomplish a specific objective without them getting mindful of any outside influence or compulsion.

## Difference Between Manipulation and Persuasion?

The distinction among control and influence lies at their very center and the components that make them what they are. As we learned in the past part, influence is the way toward changing somebody's convictions, considerations or emotions so as to pick up their help or get them to make a specific move. The definitions sound practically indistinguishable, so how would you differentiate among influence and control when various strategies are recognizable and being utilized around you? Influence and control can now and then be befuddled as a similar idea or two of a kind. Actually, at their center, influence and control are two totally extraordinary mental strategies that can be utilized for both constructive and adverse outcomes, contingent upon the individual utilizing them and how they choose to profit by them. Influence is one strategy that can be utilized to empower somebody into making a move they were opposing or against from the start. This is regularly done through giving somebody realities about the circumstance being referred to, for example, reminding your companion they need to work in the first part of the day when it begins to get late at a get-together and they are arriving at a state of over inebriation.

Control then again, is a progression of methods and strategies shaped into a deliberately spread out arrangement to get somebody (or a gathering of individuals) to change their musings, sentiments or practices. Meanings of control regularly incorporate words like shrewd and capable, alluding to the insidious, corrupt and crafty nature of the individuals who practice this kind of Dark Psychology.

## What Is Covert Manipulation?

Clandestine Manipulation, similar to Covert Persuasion, is regularly characterized as the strategies and systems controllers utilize that can't be distinguished or even perceived right now due to their unobtrusively or because of the individual abilities of the controller themselves. A few people take up control as their calling, regularly winding up in criminal or mentally harming (to themselves as well as other people) attempts that harden their notoriety for being Master Manipulators as they impeccable their aptitudes, capacities, and assortment of compelling systems.

## Dim Psychology: What Is Dark Manipulation?

Dim Manipulation takes the obscure and regularly wicked thought processes of general and clandestine control procedures and mixes them with different strategies, hypotheses and parts of Dark Psychology with the aim of making hurt others, making confusion in their condition and doing as such for reasons going from their own pleasure and amusement to their own advantage and advancement. It tends to be hard to see the distinction (here and there unthinkable, contingent upon the methods utilized and the ability of the person at utilizing them to control others) and is regularly possibly recognized afterward when the casualties of control need to confront results of their activities and choices or are attempting to recoup from antagonistic repercussions of the circumstance they were controlled into or inside.

# The Characteristics of a Master Manipulator:

The most ideal approach to have the option to shield yourself from being the objective of control is to realize how to detect a Master Manipulator before they find the opportunity to make you simply one more casualty of their self-serving plans. Most manipulative individuals incline toward the unpretentious and determined methodology. These individuals frequently give indications of psychopathy, sociopathy, and narcissism. There is additionally a littler, however similarly malignant gathering of Master Manipulators who grasp progressively forceful (once in a while brutal) control systems that are anything but difficult to spot when experienced, yet the trouble with this sort of control is that when an individual is sufficiently striking to utilize evident control techniques on another person, that individual is as of now excessively profoundly associated with the controller or their arrangement to have the option to split away without fortuitous outcomes like repercussions busy working or cracking of the home life or individual harm (genuinely, intellectually, sincerely or mentally). The dismal truth is that paying little mind to which sort of Master Manipulator individuals wind up facing, when most control unfortunate casualties understand that something isn't right, it is past the point where it is possible to get away from the circumstance without setting aside some effort to recuperate or remake their lives and connections.

One of the most outstanding qualities of a Master Manipulator is their capacity to structure and hole up behind mental covers so as to win individuals' trust or make some shared view for an apparently more profound passionate association with the objective from their perspective.

Mental covers regularly begin to shape during adolescence and other significant changes in life when individuals begin to adjust parts of their character (purposely or accidentally). By adulthood, the vast majority are beginning to get through their own veils through expanded mindfulness, more noteworthy passionate development, mental dependability, and adjusted social aptitudes and capacities rehearsed for an incredible duration to this point. Except if, obviously, the individual has purposefully shaped a mental cover to wear as a method for controlling others.

Here is a more intensive glance at several the most widely recognized Psychological Personality Masks culminated and worn by those considering the specialty of control:

**The People Pleaser:** People Pleasers base their principal assessment of themselves on how others see, depict and feel about them. Rather than shaping their own suppositions and voicing them around others, they tune in and concur with the prevalent attitudes shared by everyone around them so they generally have companions and strong associations paying little heed to where they are.

Controllers make this to the following stride and put their People pleaser cover on to concur with everybody they converse with, particularly on the off chance that they need the individual they're prevailing upon to accomplish something for them. This can be a perilous strategy for controllers with enormous groups of friends or gatherings of individuals around them (from colleagues to loved ones). It turns out to be considerably more hazardous when the individuals around them are differing and dwells on furthest edges of the range with regards to picking their sides on some random subject. On the off chance that the controller concurs with one individual and, at that point is heard concurring with another person of the contrary conclusion, they've recently caught themselves in a circumstance where they can be viewed as a liar and lose the trust they depend on so strongly so as to get individuals to do what they need.

**The Hero Mask:** This is a more straightforward and surer veil that controllers wear. The individuals who wear this cover need to feel like the saint or the person who is required in some random circumstance and is normal in the expert world. In any case, controllers flourish with having others get things done for them so the ones who additionally have a courage complex (and can deal with the two effectively) have built up their own techniques for being viewed as the saint and getting the kudos for achievements while persuading everyone around them to accomplish all the work. The advantage of this is they can fill jobs that are gainful to how others see them and their own prosperity when an objective is met or an undertaking is done successfully.

This sort of cover can likewise be flipped by experienced controllers normally wear the Hero veil when conditions are certain and occasions play out the manner in which they proposed with their impact. On account of the human component of the circumstance (through and through freedom, defects and passionate reactions) there is constantly an opportunity that a control method will reverse discharge, regardless of how well it was arranged or executed. At the point when this occurs, the accomplished controller knows to flip their Hero veil to uncover the contrary side of its inclination, the Martyr cover. This side of the cover paints the wearer as the unfortunate casualty so as to draw feel sorry for and occupy consideration from their job throughout occasions or as an approach to reduce the seriousness of their ramifications for disappointment. For controllers, this side of the veil has been planned not exclusively to gain feel sorry for yet to totally move duty regarding the failings on the individual they were controlling. They assume the fault; the controller is given another opportunity or excused dependent on their absence of command over the other individual's activities (most definitely) and the controller has quite recently added another helpful experience to their general information and practice of Dark Manipulation using Psychological Personality covers.

Because of their requirement for control, the individuals who were named controllers mentally will in general incline toward their own organization or make a gathering of individuals around them that have lower certainty or are increasingly thoughtful. This implies it is uncommon to discover a gathering of manipulative individuals cooperating. Another explanation behind this is Master Manipulators are regularly just worried in their own advantage and advancement paying little mind to the damage it might do to other people, despite the fact that they need that individual or those individuals so as to accomplish their definitive objective, whatever that may be at that point. Controllers will in general be attracted to authority positions since they have an ability for getting individuals to do whatever they are advised or welcome to participate on, as long as it doesn't put the manipulative individual at any hazard or compromise their remaining in the earth (regardless of whether it is work, home or in social settings).

# *Chapter #6*

# *Well known Manipulation*

# *Techniques*

At the point when Master Manipulators target others for passionate, sentimental or other social purposes and discover somebody they are prepared to do something amazing for, their initial step is to win their trust and establish the frameworks of individual association. Despite the fact that they are shallow on the manipulative individual, their objective will have no questions that they really feel the feelings they portray or thinking the contemplations they are partaking so as to pick up and hold their trust. This is a typical and dull characteristic among the entirety of the characters, ruthless sorts, controllers and different gatherings of individuals whose activities and practices have become the investigation of Dark Psychology. Since their objectives and goals require the help of others who don't understand they are being impacted and controlled, the primary strategies Master Manipulators need to investigate, pick and flawless through commonsense use are the ones that emphasis on winning individuals' trust through double dealing and influence, all while appearing as real or more board as could be expected under the circumstances.

## Genius Tip: Become an Observer:

All Master Manipulators are eyewitnesses. Indeed, even individuals who may not be viewed as manipulative ordinarily (however utilize strategies for control in their day by day lives or have utilized or depended on them before) know the significance of waiting and observing how others associate with the individuals around them, in different conditions or in their particular settings. Increasing a comprehension of how their objectives think, feel, respond and communicate with others is basic to the arrangement of a viable control plan.

Seeing before reaching gives Master Manipulators the data they have to know with the goal that they can:

Pick the most ideal approach to move toward their objective and make their underlying association is the individual somebody that discussions transparently and excitedly with individuals they meet? Assuming this is the case, the best introductory methodology might be the immediate one. Is the individual somebody that will in general stay away from others, especially in bigger gatherings or intuitive circumstances?

Provided that this is true, the patient methodology may be better. Rather than strolling up and presenting themselves, a virtual greeting to espresso through web-based life or by work email might be their best choice after the objective has known them for in any event a couple of days (sufficiently long to begin getting settled around them). Pick the privilege Psychological Personality Mask to wear around them to support their collaboration or intimidation into getting all the more profoundly included do the activities of the objective or the manner in which they address others propose that they are the sort of individual should be required? For this kind of focus on, a Master Manipulator would no doubt put on their Victim or Helpless Mask so they can get the objective to do what they need by causing them to feel like a saint (even in spite of the fact that looking back, their words and activities will undoubtedly be deciphered as destructive). Does the objective view themselves as a greater amount of a pariah? Right now, circumstance, a manipulative individual will need to figure out how to locate some shared conviction, so the best decision for them is to likewise extend the show and standards of conduct of an outsider.

For instance, everybody at the workplace cherishes hero motion pictures, including the Master Manipulator. Another colleague comes in that the manipulative individual sees as a potential objective however in watching their conduct discovers the individual isn't only somewhat timid and calm, maintaining a strategic distance from others as well as can be expected. At the point when they are brought into discussion, they experience no difficulty voicing their assessments, in any event, investing heavily in being the just one in the workplace who doesn't care for superhuman films. The best methods for approach for a Master Manipulator right now the one-on-one friendly exchange, however just away from other associates or individuals who realize they are lying when they tell the objective they additionally are over the superhuman films continually being put out. They will at that point even make this supposition a stride further as a method for charming themselves to the objective by feigning exacerbation and snickering about the network shows, books and games about superheroes and there is only no getting away. The two will share a chuckle and the association will be framed.

Since the remainder of the workplace has been put off by the new collaborator's antagonistic mentality to cordial cooperation and confident assessments about media outlets and different subjects when somebody approaches them, they have set themselves as the ideal objective for control by segregating themselves from individuals who know the Master Manipulator all around ok to caution them of the beguiling conduct before it turns into an issue or while there is as yet an opportunity for them to break liberated from their hold. From the perspective on the objective, the manipulative colleague has demonstrated they can possibly be an old buddy and earned their trust by additionally carrying on like a pariah around them.

At the same time, the Master Manipulator is cautiously observing and controlling their day by day collaborations with the goal that the objective doesn't scrutinize this view and the colleagues who have known them for quite a long time don't see an adjustment as a part of their character or conduct that would fill in as a notice that they are not who they guarantee to be. Right now, manipulative circumstance, it benefits both the Master Manipulator, their latent capacity targets and the individuals encompassing them two to tackle and depend on their forces of perception. The objective particularly, as observing the entirety of their colleagues and how they associate with each other before freeing themselves up to any of them could have forestalled their inclusion with a Master Manipulator.

Pick how best to continue so as to meet their objectives or get whatever it is that they need this implies picking the correct strategies and systems for control and framing an arrangement dependent on the entirety of the data they've accumulated. The more individualized they can make a manipulative buddy of activity for their objective, the more prominent their odds of progress.

# Different qualities of Master Manipulators:

Absence of comprehension, or seeing however absence of worry, for individual limits of any sort controllers need just absolute command over their exploited people, alongside their musings, feelings, and activity. The more they can attack and impact their own space, the more control they believe they have. Traitorousness is a major issue with manipulative individuals they will discuss functioning as a group and confronting each challenge together, saying whatever they should to keep their objectives agreeable and energetic about the arrangement. Be that as it may, the minute anything turns out badly, or somebody meddles with their prosperity, the Master Manipulator experiences no difficulty escaping to safeguard their own advantages and leaving their objective to tidy up the wreckage while assuming the fault for all disappointments or issues made by the control strategy.

Ace Manipulators appreciate focusing on great individuals (or individuals that others order as "great") Everybody has their own assessment of what establishes a decent individual, however for the most part great individuals are those with hopeful points of view, a supportive demeanor despite challenges, very much sharpened compassion and enthusiastic development and a general want to see everybody succeeding.

Great individuals are regularly the objectives of manipulative people as they are increasingly open with their correspondences and are continually ready to assist when they can. Manipulative individuals regularly depict great individuals as guileless and trusting, two-character characteristics they search for in their exploited people, as it makes them simpler to exploit. Contingent upon their own thought processes or plan, manipulative individuals can target great individuals only for the test of getting them to accomplish something awful (subsequent to being persuaded it is the privilege or just alternative) and the pleasure in seeing them battle with their assessment of themselves when they understand what they've done. This is a typical practice for manipulative individuals who blossom with turmoil, especially if their own life has taken a stale or exhausting turn.

## Instructions to Protect Yourself from A Manipulator:

It is regularly said that activities express stronger than words. With regards to shielding yourself from control, figuring out how to pass judgment on the nature of the individuals around you or the individuals you come into contact with by how they carry on in various circumstances or with various individuals over the things they state is the best exhortation anybody can get. Manipulative individuals are the meaning of "deceptive" and the best method to abstain from getting maneuvered into their childish plans, requirement for bedlam and self-delight over whatever else is to not be tricked by their deliberately picked words.

Master Manipulators or any individual who utilizes manipulative methods for their own advantage or pleasure is to consistently be addressing. This doesn't imply that it is best not to confide in individuals all in all. While numerous individuals will attempt to control others sooner or later in their lives, most of individuals have been appeared by brain research and through long periods of character, study to be generally legitimate and open when they are attempting to frame an association with someone else or set up their place inside a gathering of individuals. A great many people need to be enjoyed and regarded for who they are at their center so they don't need to put on veils or recall lies about what they do and don't care for with various individuals. This is something that manipulative individuals exploit when they are chasing for targets and the normal want to confide in others that a great many people experience is additionally the ruin of many. To abstain from getting one of those individuals who sees everything unmistakably looking back in the wake of seeing through a manipulative activity or confronting the outcomes of having a functioning job in a Master Manipulator's arrangement, start heeding your gut feelings and posing inquiries when you have concerns. Be energized whenever new open doors come your direction yet make certain to do your examination before tolerating an offer, making a plunge or obliging another person's arrangement. Make new companions and experience associating with individuals however find a workable pace as much as you can by observing them from others' perspectives and tuning in to how they converse with and about others.

On the off chance that you ever become worried about your considerations, emotions and activities and are not sure with respect to why (especially on the off chance that it is something you would have told somebody you could never think, feel or do), make a stride back and investigate what you feel, why you are addressing yourself, who else is associated with what's caught your consideration, and build up how you feel about your job in all things. In case you're feeling that something is off or amiss with what's going on around you, there in all probability is and the best way to recover control when you wind up trapped in a manipulative snare is to:

Watch the circumstance and make sense of what explicitly isn't right Determine who is included and who is doing the controlling Remove yourself from the circumstance, looking for help from others if vital stop contact with the manipulative individual, announcing them to the specialists or to a legitimate figure (like a business or administrator) if the circumstance is sufficiently extreme to require further or conceivably legitimate activity.

## What Is Hypnosis and How Does It Work?

Enchanting may have various usages that can be utilized with various degrees of achievement depending upon a person's motivation and extraordinary goals for it as a psychological organization gadget. At its most fundamental level, hypnotizing is portrayed as an accommodating movement taken by a readied stupor inducer and someone else with the desire for helping that person with better understanding their own mental and energetic states.

Trancelike impact has attaches driving right back to pre-Christianity days in Persia, Greek, Central Europe, and the Middle East when it was used as a procedure for reflection for a couple and focused as a significant kind of prescription by others. Leaders of the time were acknowledged to have recovering forces and would perform formal entrancing philosophy and methods on their lovers to fix sicknesses from headaches to terrible dreams and physical torments that were totally mental. Some have portrayed it as a sort of otherworldly drug while others receive an inexorably reasonable methodology and clutch it as a trance like express that opens the mind in habits that individuals can't achieve without any other person. In their decisions, when the mind is open along these lines (through feasible stupor and the bearing of a readied trance inducer), man can show up at levels of individual comprehension and cognizance of across the board laws past what is attainable when they are in their ordinary step by step mental and enthusiastic state. On account of this conviction, various pros in hypnotizing have submitted their lives and occupations to the mission for extra data through trancelike impact and reflection, endeavoring to open disguised regions of the cerebrum (for the people who acknowledge that individuals simply use a little section of our mental

restrain yet can rise to our most extreme limit through rest actuating frameworks).

FUN FACT: The examination of enchanting and a part of the more powerful techniques and systems were made by a man named Franz Mesmer of Austria who was known for putting on a dark wizard's cover, playing fragile, anyway odd music during his daze gatherings and using magnets to help partner people to their higher temper. These extraordinary and formal practices are a bit of why various people consider charm and serenades when they consider subliminal treatment as opposed to its focal points as a medicinal gadget. Franz Mesmer is moreover the inspiration driving "mesmerizing". To entrance someone means to thoroughly draw and hold their thought or place for some time. Right when someone or something is hypnotizing then he, she or it can get someone's thought and obsession while moreover animating notions of marvel or effortlessness. This word as often as possible goes straightforwardly by entrancing in people's minds when the subject comes up. There are colossal measures of points of interest that have been associated with daze that has driven it to be used for an arrangement of purposes:

Therapeutic entrancing can be used in the treatment of physical torment decline for people who are in recovery after a physical issue or encountering a consistent infection. It can in like manner be used in the treatment of troublesome or wrecking diseases that have no discernable clinical explanation anyway have been associated with mental enrollment of signs and disorder Hypnosis has been seemed to help with recovery from addictions, for instance, alcohol misuse and dependence on harder prescriptions. It can in like manner be used to stop routine practices like shopping to the point of indebtedness or shock the officials passes that lead to enthusiastic changes.

In the mid-1800s, hypnotizing was also purportedly used as a strategy for sedation before clinical methodology or while treating patients with troublesome reactions. One of the most broadly perceived disarrays about hypnotizing is that the individual being entranced is going under the total mental control of their assistant and giving up their ability to choose decisions or control their exercises. While the laid-back mental state made through enchanting frameworks makes people progressively helpless against impact and subliminal effect, the individual doing the entrancing has no genuine control over the person's exercises. One explanation this is such a comprehensively acknowledged assurance is that the fault of spellbinding methodology has normally been used by people who have suffer religions and mental oppressor social affairs. While there is minimal evidence that stupor truly can make people take exercises they would not do all alone, for instance, check out a bank burglary or sneak a delicate into a structure, it is a renowned explanation since it empties commitment in regards to the individual who is certainly fought with enduring, perceiving or unveiling their lead to a court or to their loved ones. The essential explanation behind a daze pro isn't to participate as an essential concern control strategy once their subject is totally enchanted, yet rather to go about as a guide through them withdrew and united state of mental center intrigue.

There are an immense number of different entrancing systems that someone can peruse to find the best methodologies for managing their issues or showing up at their own or master objectives. Put a smart request in on the web and there are numerous pages of results that surface, each one declaring to have information on the best hypnotizing procedures, practices, and exercises for people expecting to consider the workmanship. With such a critical number of decisions for how to push toward daze in this way various people expecting to grant their own flourishing to others, various people end up endeavoring the underlying hardly any they find and halting when those underlying relatively few systems don't work for their individual needs.

The best way to deal with not respect the staggering heap of all that data is to take an inexorably drew in or confined system. But on the off chance that you live in an amazingly unassuming network or a separated zone, analyze shows that most typical American towns have in any occasion three to five unmistakable counselors or examiners open for interviews on any extent of mental concerns. In towns where there is a tremendous mental region in the clinical system, people looking for information on mental hypnotizing techniques and theories have a predominant chance of finding a power that has firsthand understanding or approved planning in medicinal daze. For the people who don't have an immense decision of mental masters to contact in their general region, each and every approved investigator have contributed some vitality thinking about therapeutic entrancing in the journey for their degrees. Regardless of whether you are planning to be hypnotized as a kind of treatment, whether or not you have requests concerning the darker side of mental stupor or whether you just need to get some answers concerning the subject when everything is said in done, a specialist will have the alternative to address your requests and even make recommendations about resulting stages or where to search for feasible experience openings. Whether or not you would lean toward not to be hypnotized, someone who has considered the hypotheses or cleaned it themselves are the best wellspring of data and information that anyone excited about getting some answers concerning Dark Psychology and stupor could ever ask for!

Enchanting works by following a meticulously spread out methodology that can be adjusted (if crucial) by the people who have thought about their picked frameworks and have experience dealing with potential challenges that rise with entrancing someone. It is basic to recollect that few out of every odd individual is a better than average opportunities for daze systems, believe it or not, under 20% of the masses responds to hypnotizing as they would have wanted to go into their first gathering. The reason behind this is in light of the fact that enchanting is only a technique for making someone progressively open to affect. Any person who has compelling energetic, mental or mental deterrents is increasingly loath to be productive as the subject of entrancing while the people who have negligible enthusiastic improvement or experience to have framed their psychology, for instance, kids and those with perspectives that impact their ability to control their thoughts and sentiments, are largely the more helpfully affected into trancelike states in view of the intriguing and pleasing condition made each time a hypnotizing meeting starts.

## Different Types of Hypnosis Techniques:

The underlying advance to any kind of enchanting is to check that the target or the part is someone that starting at now acknowledges that hypnotizing genuinely works. If the individual being enchanted is someone that thinks stupor is a joke or a mute that people use for remarkable redirection then it is profoundly improbable that psychological entrancing will be productive, in case it has any effect at all on their mental and energetic focal point of being. The people who endeavor to use hypnotizing as a Dark Persuasion or Dark Manipulation device will check for centers around that starting at now talk earnestly about enchanting or people that may not totally put confidence in its abilities yet also don't have any inspiration to vulnerability and need to acknowledge that it works. Having the individual being hypnotized tolerating that daze is the reaction for them is the hardest bit of the battle.

# Dark Psychology and Human Nature:

Other Techniques at Work All Around Us Dark Psychology is one of the most exact and honest portrayals of human instinct accessible for study, assortment and advancement into handy aptitudes. There are a variety of strategies that can be read and polished for the individuals who are keen on finding out about and acing Dark Psychology.

The individuals who like to utilize Dark Psychology and related strategies on others for their own advantage do so on the grounds that they realize how to as well as get satisfaction from going after individuals' acceptable characteristics. One procedure that can be utilized for this reason for existing is the craft of enchantment, which can be for sentimental or manipulative last objectives. By focusing on individuals' acceptable assessments of themselves like their affection for their own style or their high assessment of their own appearance, the individuals who use enchantment as a weapon can procure people groups' trust (regularly through commendations and boosting their vanity) before getting them to come nearer either genuinely or truly so as to get them to do or accept what they state. Sex can be an amazing and perilous helper for both the individual utilizing it as a control method and for the individual being controlled. One approach to shield yourself from engaging with enchanting controllers is to rehearse self-care consistently, paying little mind to the length of the relationship, on the grounds that when you quit contemplating and looking equitably (or as dispassionately as conceivable thinking about that connections beginning with enticement frequently construct compelling passionate ties or associations that can be utilized for both impact and control in an inappropriate hands).

Sweet talk can be an incredible and successful device for the individuals who depend on their insight into others, how their feelings structure and venture, and their particular character types so as to control their considerations, conclusions, and activities. However that takes a great deal of training to ace for various reasons yet utilizing blandishment to get what you need is a typical practice among scalawags to eager social climbers hoping to advance up the administration chain at their organization. This method is especially famous with individuals that likewise show narcissistic and vain characteristics as these individuals appreciate observing how others respond to their positive remarks despite the fact that they realize that there is no substance to them.

For the individuals who are intrigued rehearsing bootlicking as a mental impact procedure, a great many people who have long periods of experience would prescribe for fledglings to begin their preparation to do it with outsiders like the individual behind the register at the coffeehouse or somebody they find on the road that they have never observed. They pick individuals what their identity is as of now expected to be amicable with because of the guidelines of neighborly society, yet that they don't really need to collaborate with again on the off chance that they bumble or humiliate themselves over the span of sharpening their bootlicking abilities.

To abstain from succumbing to adulation as a mental control device it is significant for people to attempt to stay target when accepting commendations, especially on the off chance that they appear to be appearing suddenly or in the event that they are originating from somebody that the individual is new to this kind of method makes what is regularly alluded to as a vanity trap. Vanity traps are fruitful for the individuals who have great relationship building abilities in light of the fact that the individual doing the complimenting first forms a situation of solace and trust and afterward supports their objective's certainty with praises or other positive articulations. This strategy goes after everybody's base should be preferred and to like themselves by realizing that others ponder them since everybody battles with being kept down by and encountering these feelings sooner or later in their lives, everybody is vulnerable to being focused for vanity traps by the individuals who have figured out how to use sweet talk as a mental weapon of control and impact over others

## What Is Reverse Psychology?

Switch Psychology is the demonstration of empowering somebody into a specific idea or activity by supporting a conflicting proclamation or conviction. This logical inconsistency fills in as a method for inspiration as the individual the Reverse Psychology strategy is being utilized on now feels they have something to demonstrate or feels they have to prevail so as to restore the logical inconsistency to the individual who at first conveyed it. It is frequently utilized as a device for comedic purposes as it very well may be a reason for false impressions for the individuals who are not comfortable or OK with the nuances of language and tone.

The means to acing and adequately utilizing Reverse psychology are basic and can best be clarified through a model:

Somebody invests the greater part of their energy censuring and talking down about the ascent of electric vehicles. In spite of their advantage to the earth, this individual won't get in one since they have such an awful assessment of them, favoring their huge gas swallowing vehicle. At the point when the opportunity arrives for them to get another vehicle, they discover one that they like the vibe of and have perused positive audits of throughout recent months. Notwithstanding, further research uncovers that it is an electrically fueled vehicle. Because of his negative perspective on electrical autos, he won't consider stepping through it for an exam drive and rather settles on another enormous gas guzzler that is progressively costly on the month to month spending plan and somewhat out of his value run. His better half anyway prefers the electrical vehicle he at first took a gander at however realizes that he will won't talk about it despite the fact that it will assist with diminishing their month to month costs. Rather than adopting the intelligent strategy and dissuading him, she chooses to attempt Reverse Psychology so he alters his perspective on the electric vehicle and does as such while never scrutinizing that it was totally his thought. Rather than disclosing to him how much better it would be for them, she discusses everything that additional cash could be going to and guaranteeing that she wouldn't fret doing without. Right now, will be presently utilizing Reverse Psychology strategies as well as other Dark Psychology methods, for example, aloof hostility (when she speaks by implication about abandoning due to all the cash they spend on gas for the bigger vehicles) and negative idea control (when she begins to make reference to the entirety of the terrible parts of the bigger vehicles and lining them up with comments like, "However who thinks about that?" all together to ingrain coerce and support him enthusiastically that makes her look all the more well on him and their circumstance.

Regardless of what your enthusiasm for Dark Psychology and the various procedures, practices, and structures it can take, we trust you've made the most of our guide and need to urge everybody one to continue scanning for data and learn constantly! That is the way headways and revelations like the ones remembered for this book are discovered, shaped, consummated and put to use in viable conditions in all parts of human life.

# Characteristics of a Narcissistic and Aggressive Person

1.      Grandiose feeling of pretentiousness

Pretentiousness is one of the characterizing characteristics of a narcissistic individual. Pomposity is something beyond vanity or self-importance; it is having an unreasonable feeling of predominance. Narcissists accept they are "uncommon and exceptional and that solitary other unique individuals can get them. They just need to be related just as partner themselves with others, spots, or things of high status. Narcissists additionally accept that nobody is better than them and that they ought to be perceived in any event, when they have done literally nothing to gain acknowledgment. They will frequently lie or misrepresent their abilities or accomplishments. What's more, when they talk about connections or work, all you will hear is the secret extraordinary they are, the amount they contribute, or how fortunate individuals are to have them in their lives.

2.      Sense of privilege

Since they see themselves as one of a kind and exceptional, narcissistic consistently hope to be given good treatment. They truly accept that they ought to get anything they desire. They likewise expect that everybody ought to naturally follow every one of their desires and the ones who don't in their eyes are futile. And furthermore, the ones who set out to ask something consequently or completely oppose their will ought to set themselves up for shock, animosity or the brush off.

3.      Needs steady acclaim and deference

The feeling of prevalence in a narcissist resembles an inflatable that needs a constant flow of acknowledgment and acclaim to keep it expanded; without it, it continuously loses air. A periodic commendation isn't sufficient. Narcissistic individuals need steady commendations to take care of their inner self, and in this way, they will in general encircle themselves with individuals who might do only that. Such sorts of connections are generally uneven in light of the fact that it is constantly about what they get and not what they give. What's more, on the off chance that they feel like their admirer has decreased their consideration and acclaim or altogether quit offering it, they would regard that as a selling out.

4.      Exploits others without blame or disgrace

Narcissistic individuals do not have the capacity to distinguish themselves with the sentiments of others, that is, to placed themselves into "others' point of view." This implies they need sympathy. Normally, a large number of the individuals in their lives are seen as articles that are there to serve their requirements. What's more, because of that, they would exploit others without reconsidering as long as they get what they need. While these relational abuses are normally just self-evident, once in a while they can be inside and out malevolent. Narcissists basically don't have the capacity to consider how individuals are getting influenced by their practices. Also, some of the time, in any event, when it gets brought up, they would at present not get it. Getting their own needs met is the main thing they comprehend.

5.      Lives in a dreamland that underpins their hallucinations of loftiness

Reality will never bolster narcissists' pretentious sentiments of themselves; along these lines, as a spread, they live in a dreamland loaded up with mysterious reasoning, self-duplicity, and bending. They have dreams of praising themselves of perfect love, engaging quality; splendor, power, and boundless achievement that cause them to feel in charge and uncommon. Having such dreams shields them from having sentiments of disgrace and internal vacancy; in this manner, conclusions and realities that repudiate them are either excused away or disregarded. Anything that represents a risk to their dream bubble is typically met with wrath or extraordinary protectiveness.

6.   Frequently deprecates, menaces, threatens or disparages others

Narcissistic and forceful people consistently feel compromised when they run over an individual who seems to have something that they don't have – particularly the individuals who have certainty and ubiquity. They additionally feel undermined by individuals who challenge them in any capacity and the person who aren't agreeable towards them. Most occasions, they would fall back on putting these individuals down as an approach to kill the danger – disdain is the resistance system. This should be possible in a pompous or disparaging manner to show how little these individuals intend to them. What's more, different occasions, they may decide to go on the assault with dangers, harassing, ridiculing, and affront to constrain that individual to get once more into line. The kinds of harsh individuals

## 1.    The narcissistic abuser

The narcissist is fixated on self, they continually consider self, they venerate self, photos self, advances self, takes a gander at self and all the more critically, they need others to do all these as well. A narcissist is excessively worried about their picture, abilities, and looks and will do anything no make a difference the expense to maintain all these. They are likewise excessively worried about getting love and recognition. They adore and flourish in the consideration they get assuming any. They are additionally exceptionally appealing however detest having a charming or active accomplice. They feel this would take consideration from them. A narcissistic abuser is likewise exceptionally rude, self-ingested, and extremely narrow minded. When associating with others, they generally just need to discuss themselves, their achievements, abilities, agony, and shameful acts, and if the discussion movements to someone else, they are typically exhausted and impartial and just considers how to switch the discussion back to themselves.

A narcissistic abuser is something contrary to a genuinely poor abuser for the explanation that they can supplant an individual like a sweetheart whenever with someone else. This is on the grounds that they are possibly keen on a relationship of any sort just when it benefits them some way or another. They may likewise act as a decent parent to their kid for the explanation that he sees the youngster as their own "expansion." This can be named as roundabout narcissism. A narcissist accepts that life is tied in with being "upbeat" and not about "respect" regardless of whether it implies getting that joy leaves others troubled for instance, leaving a spouse for another lady without mindful if the wife and youngsters would feel torment. A narcissist likewise has different qualities of other oppressive characteristics like verbal, physical, enthusiastic, budgetary, monetary, and otherworldly maltreatment.

2.    The genuinely poor abuser

This kind of abuser regularly needs confidence and acquires self-esteem from connections – generally sentimental ones. They would attempt to disconnect their accomplice from the outside world and would get extremely envious when their accomplice invests a great deal of energy with companions or even family. They become tenacious and possessive, and they use control and blame stumbling as their best instruments. On the off chance that enthusiastic control and misuse aren't working, they resort to physical or boisterous attack just to remain quiet about the accomplice.

A genuinely poor abuser as a rule feels like they can't survive without their accomplice. They would make claims, for example, the accomplice being their perfect partner or that they were intended to be as one or even case that God has uncovered to them that they ought to be as one. They would attempt to persuade the accomplice that there is no other individual who might adore them the manner in which they do. They are normally overcome with envy just as dread of losing their accomplice. They make their accomplice answerable for their joy. These sorts of abusers are generally extremely touchy, and they cry no problem at all. Their most favored love interests are those mutually dependent individuals who are genuinely more grounded than they are and who might be pardoning, gushing, and tolerant of them. These abusers can likewise be obnoxiously, truly, monetarily, or profoundly injurious.

CPSIA information can be obtained
at www.ICGtesting.com
Printed in the USA
LVHW080926260421
685569LV00011B/894